It's more than a pregnancy. It's a religion.

by Cathy Guisewite

Selected Cartoons from
Thin thighs in thirty years
Volume II

FAWCETT CREST • NEW YORK

A Fawcett Crest Book
Published by Ballantine Books
Copyright © 1986 by Universal Press Syndicate
Cathy © is syndicated internationally by Universal Press Syndicate.

This book comprises a portion of THIN THIGHS IN THIRTY
YEARS and is reprinted by arrangement with Andrews and McMeel.

Library of Congress Catalog Card Number: 86-71301

ISBN 0-449-21433-8

Manufactured in the United States of America

First Ballantine Books Edition: May 1988

BEFORE

SCRAPE SHOVEL
SCRAPE DIG
CHIP SCRAPE

AFTER

YESTERDAY, THE INSTANT MAKEOVER. TODAY, THE AUTO MAKEOVER.

IT'S TYPICAL FOR WOMEN WHO HAVE BEEN REAL GO-GETTERS IN BUSINESS TO TURN THAT SAME PASSION ONTO THE EXPERIENCE OF PARENTING.

SOME START WITH FLASH CARDS AND MUSIC LESSONS WHEN THEIR BABY IS JUST A WEEK OLD. YOU'RE NOT GOING TO DO THAT ARE YOU, ANDREA?

START EDUCATING THE BABY A WEEK AFTER BIRTH?? DON'T BE RIDICULOUS.

WE WOULD HAVE MISSED THE WHOLE NINE MONTHS OF PREGNANCY!

..THIS NEXT SELECTION IS FROM VIVALDI, LITTLE ONE...

GUISEWITE

HERE, LITTLE LADY...YOUR CARBURETOR'S SHOT, CAUSING GASKET LEAKS ON THE ALTERNATOR DRIVE SHAFT SLIP YOKE CYLINDER HEAD NUTS. OBVIOUSLY, THIS ALL HAS TO GO.

SEE?? YES, I SEE. THAT IS THE EXACT SAME TWITCH IRVING GETS IN HIS EYE WHEN HIS "SEMINAR" IS REALLY A WEEKEND WITH BRENDA.

EITHER COME UP WITH AN ESTIMATE THAT DOESN'T MAKE YOU SQUINT, OR I'M TOWING THIS KLUNKER ELSEWHERE!!

I KNOW NOTHING ABOUT CARS, BUT I KNOW A LOT ABOUT EYELIDS.

500 PEOPLE MUST LIVE IN MY APARTMENT BUILDING, BUT I DON'T KNOW ONE PERSON I CAN ASK FOR A RIDE WHEN MY CAR IS IN THE SHOP.

WHY HAVEN'T I MADE AN EFFORT TO MEET ANYONE ?? WHY DIDN'T I TAKE FIVE SECONDS TO SAY HELLO WHEN THEY WERE ALL SITTING AROUND THE POOL LAST SUMMER ?!

WHY? BECAUSE MY BATHING SUIT WAS OBSCENE! I COULDN'T SAY HELLO TO TOTAL STRANGERS WEARING THE HIGH-CUT LEG LOOK! NO SELF-RESPECTING WOMAN WOULD TRY TO MINGLE WHILE SQUASHED INTO FIVE INCHES OF GREEN ELASTIC!!! HAH!!

THERE ISN'T MUCH IN LIFE THAT WE CAN'T BLAME ON WOMEN'S SWIMWEAR.

6:00 AM:
5 MINUTES OF STRETCHES
15 MINUTES OF YOGA
20 MINUTES OF AEROBICS

5 MINUTES OF FACIAL ISOMETRICS
15 MINUTE BODY SCRUB
20 MINUTE WARDROBE WORKOUT
25 MINUTE MAKEOVER
15 MINUTES OF WHOLE WHEAT
AND HEADLINES

8:30 AM:
NOURISHED...OXYGENATED...
INVIGORATED...INFORMED..TONED
..AND READY TO HIT THE DESK.

SPLAT.

I WAS GOING TO HAVE ONE PIECE OF WHOLE WHEAT TOAST FOR BREAKFAST, BUT A LITTLE VOICE CONVINCED ME I'D WORK BETTER WITH EGGS, SAUSAGE AND A ROLL.

I WAS GOING TO JUST HAVE FRUIT FOR LUNCH, BUT A LITTLE VOICE CONVINCED ME I'D EAT LESS IN THE LONG RUN IF I HAD A SANDWICH AND SOUP.

I WAS GOING TO SIP ON A DIET SODA, BUT A LITTLE VOICE CONVINCED ME I NEEDED THE EXTRA CALCIUM FROM A CUP OF HOT CHOCOLATE.

NO MATTER HOW BIG I GET, I'LL NEVER FORGET THE LITTLE PEOPLE WHO MADE IT POSSIBLE.

IRVING COULD GIVE ME THIS BRACELET FOR VALENTINE'S DAY AND SAY IT REPRESENTS THE FULL CIRCLE OF OUR LOVE.

HE COULD GIVE ME THIS CALENDAR TO SHOW ALL THE DAYS HE WANTS TO SPEND WITH ME ...GLOVES TO HOLD MY HANDS.. VITAMINS FOR HOW I ENRICH HIM...A SQUASHED FLOWER FOR THE CRUSH HE HAS ON ME...

HE COULD WAD UP A PIECE OF TAPE AS A SYMBOL OF HIS ATTACHMENT OR RIP A PAPER TOWEL IN HALF AND SAY HE JUST ISN'T COMPLETE WITHOUT ME!!

IT'S ALMOST IMPOSSIBLE TO NOT GIVE ME A MEANINGFUL GIFT.

ANOTHER LEOTARD RUINS ITS WHOLE LIFE FOR FIVE SECONDS OF FUN.

CATHY, THIS IS STACEY. STACEY CALLED ME UP AND ASKED ME OUT TONIGHT. I'M INNOCENT.

STACEY, THIS IS CATHY. CATHY DROPPED OVER ON HER OWN WITH NO WARNING. I'M INNOCENT.

I AM TOTALLY INNOCENT! TWO WOMEN ARE PURSUING ME AND I AM ABSOLUTELY INNOCENT! FOR ONCE IN MY LIFE, I'M INNOCENT, INNOCENT, INNOCENT!!!

HOO BOY. DO I FEEL GUILTY.

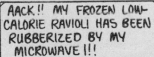

WE'VE SPENT HOURS DISCUSSING WHAT WE'LL SAY WHEN WE SEE OUR BOYFRIENDS.

WE'VE SHOPPED ALL OVER TOWN FOR NEW OUTFITS TO WEAR WHEN WE GREET OUR BOYFRIENDS... WE'VE AGONIZED OVER THE PERFECT GIFTS TO BRING OUR BOYFRIENDS...

...AND WE'VE CALCULATED THE EXACT AMOUNT OF SUN WE NEED FOR TANS THAT WILL DAZZLE OUR BOYFRIENDS.

IT TAKES A FIVE-DAY VACATION TO PREPARE FOR A FIVE-SECOND ENTRANCE.

WHEN IRVING PICKS ME UP AT THE AIRPORT, HE SITS IN HIS CAR OUTSIDE THE BAGGAGE AREA WHILE I LUG 400 POUNDS OF LUGGAGE AROUND TRYING TO FIND HIM.

WHEN ANDREA PICKS ME UP SHE SORT OF WALKS DOWN AND MEETS ME HALFWAY.

WHEN MY MOTHER PICKS ME UP, SHE CAMPS AT THE GATE FOR FOUR HOURS BEFORE THE PLANE LANDS AND SHOWERS ME WITH DEVOTION THE SECOND I GET OFF.

GREETINGS ARE IN INVERSE PROPORTION TO HOW MUCH WE'VE DONE TO DESERVE THEM.

GATE 43

THE BABY WILL BE HERE IN TWO MONTHS! HI, BABY! THIS IS DADDY!

DADDY. AACK! I'M NOT READY FOR DADDY.. AACK. NO. I'M FINE. FINE. I'VE READ THE BOOK. I'VE SEEN THE MOVIE. I'VE RENTED THE VIDEO. HA, HA. NO, FEAR IS NORMAL, HA. NO. I'M FINE. EVERYTHING IS.

..AAACK WHO ARE YOU AND WHAT IS A PREGNANT WOMAN DOING IN MY LIVING ROOM??!!

AT SEVEN MONTHS THEY START BABBLING.

HAVE YOU PAINTED THE BABY'S ROOM YET, ANDREA?

NO, BUT WE HAVE BOUGHT BABY'S FIRST ISOKINETIC WORKOUT WAGON... AN ERGO-NOMIC STROLLER... COMPACT DISC MUSICAL MOBILE... A PC WITH INTERACTIVE, PRE-VERBAL SOFTWARE... A "BUSY BOX" WITH 32-DIGIT AUTO-REDIAL...

CRIB SHEETS PRINTED WITH THE WORKS OF THE 17TH-CENTURY MASTERS.... FLASH CARDS... ENOUGH LEGO SETS TO RE-CONSTRUCT MANHATTAN...NON-TOXIC MARKERS COLOR COORDI-NATED WITH BABY'S HAND-LOOMED VCR COVER... AND A STUFFED LEMUR THAT PLAYS THE OPERAS OF PUCCINI!!

HAVE YOU PAINTED THE BABY'S CONDOMINIUM YET?

CATHY'S BEEN IN THERE DO-ING HER TAXES FOR HOURS!

IT ISN'T JUST DO-ING TAXES.

THIS IS THE ONE TIME OF THE YEAR WHEN WE'RE FORCED TO REALLY FACE FACTS AND FIND NEW WAYS TO COPE.

ACROSS THE NATION, PEOPLE ARE HUNCHED OVER DESKS TONIGHT, MAKING DISCOVER-IES THAT WILL CHANGE THEIR WHOLE LIVES...

I CAN EAT 4 "THIN MINTS" FOR ONLY 25 MORE CALORIES THAN IN 2 "DO-SI-DOS"!!

HOW COULD TAXES BE DUE NEXT WEEK, IRVING ?? HOW ?!

CATHY, WHY DOES TAX TIME ALWAYS SHOCK YOU ?!

APRIL 15 COMES EVERY YEAR! THERE ARE ADS, SIGNS, ARTICLES...WHOLE BUSINESSES DEVOTED TO APRIL 15 !

HOW COULD YOU BE ALIVE AND NOT KNOW THAT YOU'RE SUPPOSED TO DO SOMETHING ABOUT APRIL 15 ?!!

I RELATE TO TAX TIME THE WAY YOU RELATE TO VALENTINE'S DAY.

"BOSS'S DAY" IS EFFICIENTLY OVER IN ONE DAY...WHY DO YOU SUPPOSE "SECRETARIES DAY" DRAGS OUT FOR AN ENTIRE WEEK, CHARLENE??

SECRETARIES WEEK

BECAUSE IF SECRETARIES ALL CELEBRATED WITH A LONG LUNCH ON THE SAME DAY, BUSINESS WOULD BE THROWN INTO CHAOS, AND THE ECONOMIC SYSTEM OF THE ENTIRE COUNTRY WOULD COLLAPSE.

BUT WHEN BOSSES ALL TAKE A LONG LUNCH ON THE SAME DAY, NO ONE SEEMS TO NOTICE.

I HAD TO ASK.

SECRETARIES WEEK

AFTER 20 YEARS OF CHEERING WOMEN ON TO BE ALL THEY CAN BE, A STUDY WAS PUBLISHED LAST MONTH BRANDING THOSE SAME TRIUMPHANT WOMEN AS "OLD MAIDS" IF NOT MARRIED BY THEIR EARLY 30s.

WHILE THE "SPINSTER SURVEY" WAS TOO ABSURD TO BE TAKEN SERIOUSLY BY ANYONE...

...SOME PARTICULARLY ASTUTE WOMEN HAVE BEEN ABLE TO UTILIZE ITS FINDINGS AS A SPRINGBOARD FOR MEANINGFUL DIALOGUES WITH THEIR MALE COUNTERPARTS.

WHAT'S IT TO YOU, YOU OLD GEEZER?!!

SNICKER SNICKER

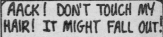

ATTENTION ALL EMPLOYEES, AND WELCOME TO THE CORPORATE SOFTBALL SEASON.

JEFF, WHO HASN'T SCORED SINCE 1983 AND IS 0-FOR-16 THIS YEAR, IS GIVING HIS BEST PITCH TO LYNN, WHO SWINGS AND JUST MISSES HIS NOSE... ...MEANWHILE, TOM AND MARY ARE WARMING EACH OTHER UP...

...WHILE JOE HAS ONCE AGAIN STRUCK OUT WITH CINDY, AND IN A BRILLIANT DOUBLE PLAY, KAREN SEEMS TO BE HEADING FOR HOME WITH BOTH TED AND BILL....

YOU'RE SUPPOSED TO BE TALKING ABOUT THE PEOPLE WHO ARE PLAYING SOFTBALL, CHARLENE.

WHAT FOR?

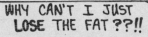

I'LL BARBECUE THE STEAKS, CATHY. YOU MAKE THE POTATO SALAD, FRUIT SALAD, CORN, COLE SLAW, ROLLS, DIPS, DRINKS AND DESSERT!

WHY DON'T I BARBECUE THE STEAKS AND YOU DO ALL THE OTHER STUFF?

NAH... I WOULDN'T WANT YOU TO GET ALL DIRTY.

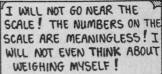

EVERY YEAR I TORTURE MY-SELF ABOUT ALL THE THINGS I BUY TRYING TO GET BEAU-TIFUL FOR SUMMER.

DRESSES TO MAKE ME LOOK THIN... MAKEUP TO MAKE ME LOOK TAN... SUNGLASSES TO MAKE ME LOOK COOL... WHY... WHY... WHY...

FOR ONCE IN MY LIFE I'M JUST GOING TO RELAX THIS YEAR AND ACCEPT MYSELF AS I AM.

VAIN.

THAT WILL BE $72.50.

summer fashions

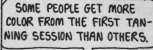

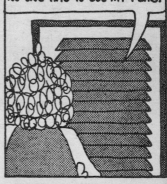

YOU HAVEN'T EVEN PLANNED ANDREA'S SHOWER YET ??

NAH... THERE'S PLENTY OF TIME.

HER BABY'S DUE IN THREE WEEKS, CATHY! IT'S NORMAL FOR WOMEN WHO ARE CONFUSED ABOUT MOTHERHOOD TO EXPRESS SOME DENIAL, BUT...

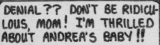

DENIAL ?? DON'T BE RIDICULOUS, MOM! I'M THRILLED ABOUT ANDREA'S BABY !!

WHAT BABY ?

OF 117 DEMOCRATIC NATIONS IN THE WORLD, THE UNITED STATES IS THE ONLY ONE WITH NO GUARANTEED MATERNITY LEAVE.

INCREDIBLE!

BABY CONGRATULATIONS

A NEW MOTHER'S "OPTIONS" ARE: GET FIRED, GO BROKE, OR COLLAPSE FROM EXHAUSTION.

EVEN THE SOVIET UNION GIVES A 6-MONTH LEAVE WITH FULL PAY!

UNTIL BUSINESSES QUIT TREATING PARENTING AS A HOBBY, WE'RE DOOMING OURSELVES TO A NATION OF FRUSTRATED, GUILTY ADULTS AND RAISING WHOLE GENERATIONS OF BABIES WHO NEVER EVEN HAD THE BONDING OF A 24-HOUR PARENT IN THE FIRST PRECIOUS WEEKS OF LIFE!!

HOW I LOVE THE GIGGLING AND GABBING OF A BABY SHOWER!

COME IN

...A BLUE AND PINK RATTLE. NO. ALL WRONG. THE RODS AND CONES OF A NEWBORN'S EYES HAVE NOT MATURED ENOUGH TO PERCEIVE COLOR VALUES.

...A STATIONARY SEAT. NO GOOD. NO WAY. A BABY NEEDS LINEAR ROCKING TO STIMULATE NEUROMUSCULAR COORDINATION AND WEIGHT GAIN.

...SILENT DUCK MOBILE. WRONG, WRONG, WRONG! DON'T PEOPLE KNOW TOYS HAVE TO STIMULATE BOTH THE RIGHT AND LEFT SIDES OF THE BRAIN TO PROMOTE INTELLIGENCE?!!

WHAT GIFTS DO YOU WANT FOR YOUR BABY, ANDREA?

OH, ANYTHING WOULD BE WONDERFUL!

THE '80s WOMAN ARRIVES AT THE MATERNITY WARD LIKE A ONE-WOMAN BIRTHING BRIGADE.

U-HAUL

MATERNITY

SHE'S STUDIED DOZENS OF BOOKS, GONE TO CLASSES, ATTENDED SEMINARS, SEEN FILMS, MEMORIZED CHARTS, AND TRAINED LIKE AN OLYMPIC ATHLETE FOR 9 MONTHS.

MATERNITY

ACUTELY AWARE OF WHAT EVERY SINGLE CELL IN HER BODY IS DOING, SHE TENSES WITH ANIMAL INSTINCT FOR THE BIGGEST CHALLENGE OF HER LIFE....

ADMISSIONS DESK

...TRYING TO CONVINCE SOMEONE SHE'S HAVING A BABY.

NAH..GO ON HOME. YOU DON'T LOOK READY YET.

ADMISSIONS

Guisewite

THE ONLY ONE WHO DOESN'T AUTOMATICALLY CRY AT A BIRTH IS THE BABY.

IT'S SHOVED FROM ITS COZY NEST... SPENDS HOURS BEING SQUASHED THROUGH A BIRTH CANAL... AND IS WELCOMED BY A ROOM OF SOBBING GIANTS WHO CUT OFF ITS LIFE SUPPORT SYSTEM.

REMARKABLY, THE BABY'S FIRST INSTINCT IS NOT A CRY, BUT A LOOK OF UTTER AMAZEMENT....

THIS HAD BETTER BE GOOD.